Beautiful Melodies

FOR BEGINNING PIANO SOLO

ISBN 978-1-70517-518-7

HAL•LEONARD®

Visit Hal Leonard Online at
www.halleonard.com

World headquarters, contact:
Hal Leonard
7777 West Bluemound Road
Milwaukee, WI 53213
Email: info@halleonard.com

In Europe, contact:
Hal Leonard Europe Limited
1 Red Place
London, W1K 6PL
Email: info@halleonardeurope.com

In Australia, contact:
Hal Leonard Australia Pty. Ltd.
4 Lentara Court
Cheltenham, Victoria, 3192 Australia
Email: info@halleonard.com.au

At the Ivy Gate

Written by BRIAN CRAIN

Moderately slow

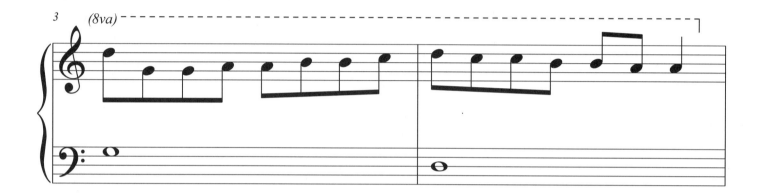

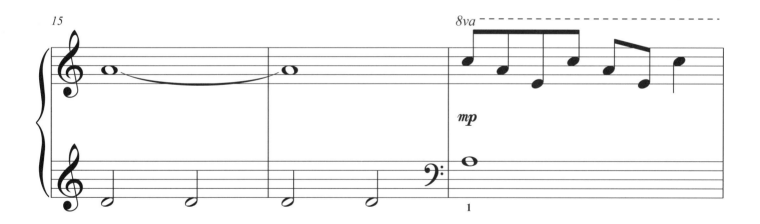

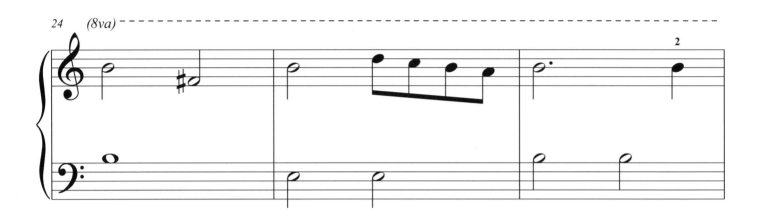

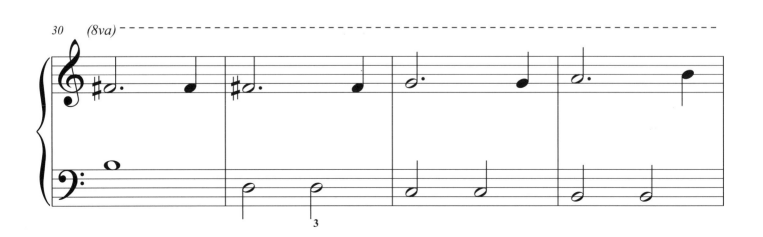

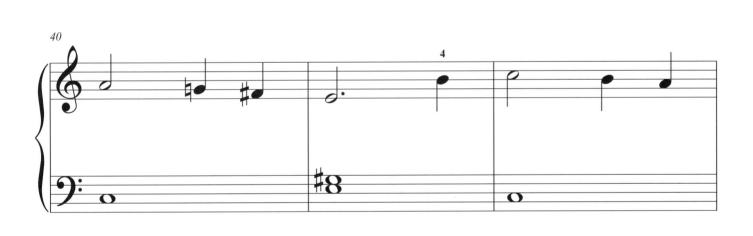

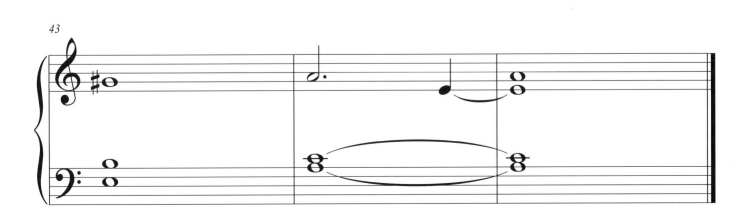

Comptine d'un autre été: L'après-midi

from AMÉLIE

By YANN TIERSEN

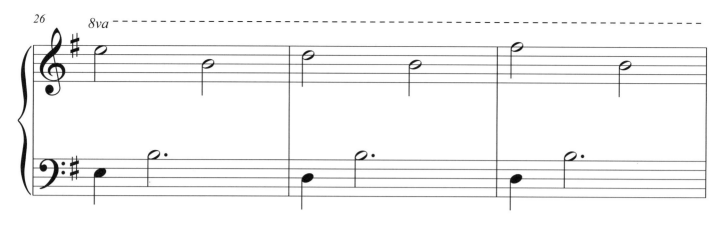

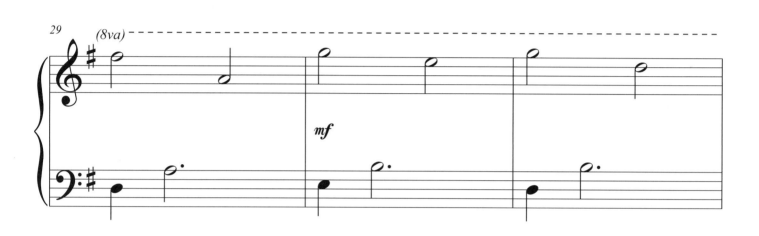

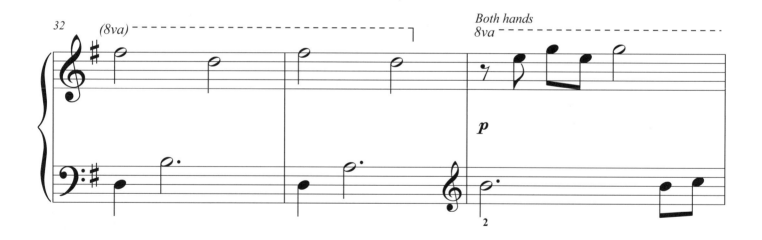

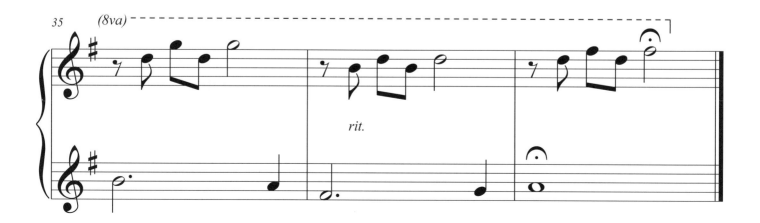

A Day Without Rain

By ENYA and NICKY RYAN

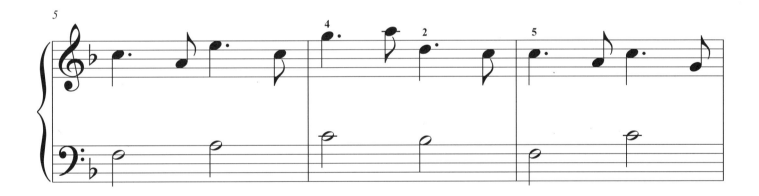

For the Love of a Princess

from the Twentienth Century Fox Motion Picture BRAVEHEART

Music by JAMES HORNER

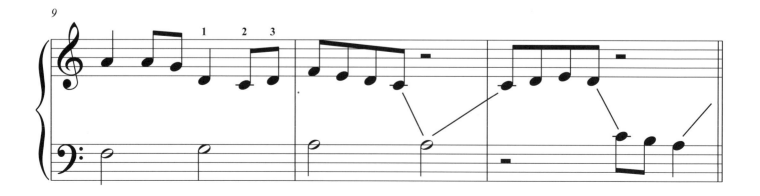

Slightly faster

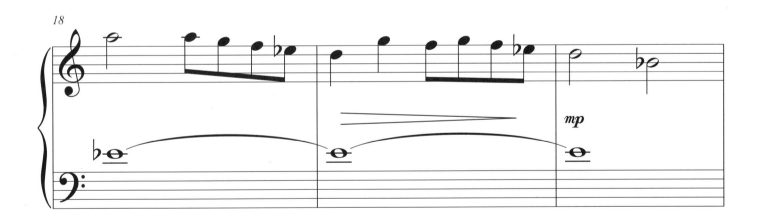

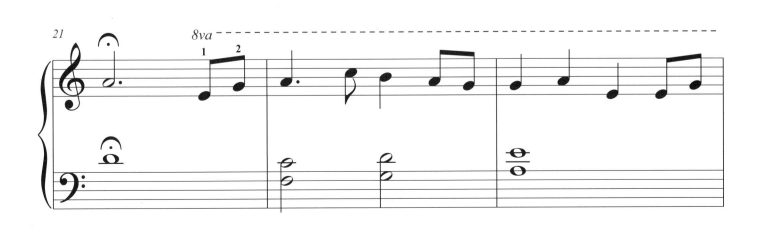

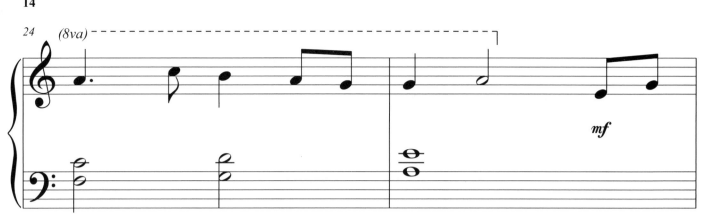

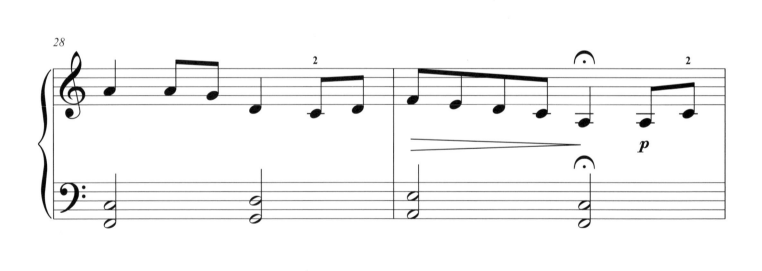

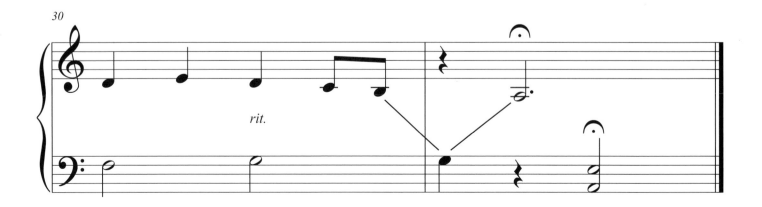

Hymn

By LIZ STORY

Moderately

Fine

17

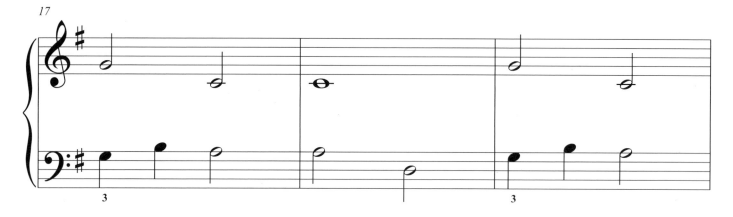

20

23

26

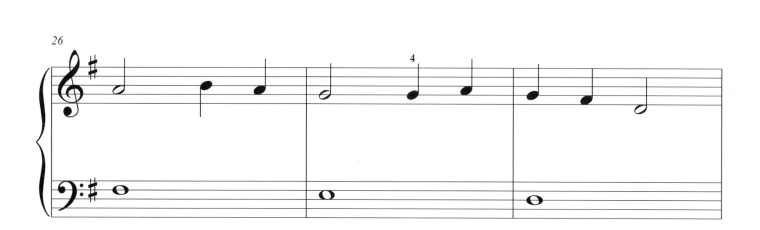

D.C. al Fine

Imagine

Words and Music by
JOHN LENNON

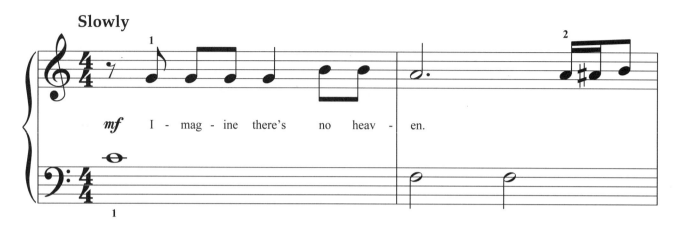

Slowly

mf I - mag - ine there's no heav - en.

It's eas - y if you try._____ No hell be - low

us, a - bove us on - ly sky.

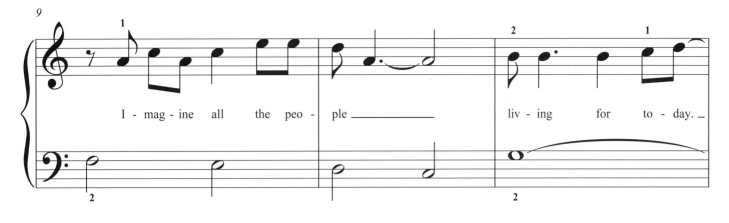

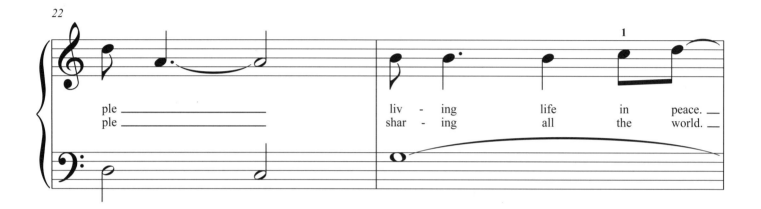

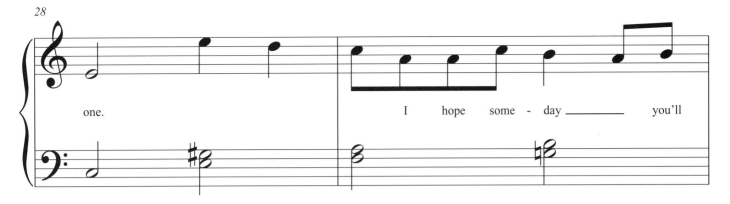

one.   I hope some - day _____ you'll

1.

join   us _____   and   the   world _____   will

be   as   one.   I - mag - ine   no   pos - ses -

2.

and   the   world _____   will   be   as   one.

La Valse d'Amélie
from AMÉLIE

By YANN TIERSEN

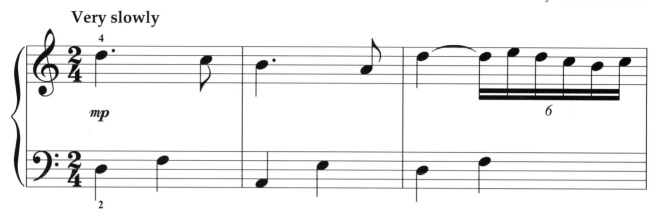

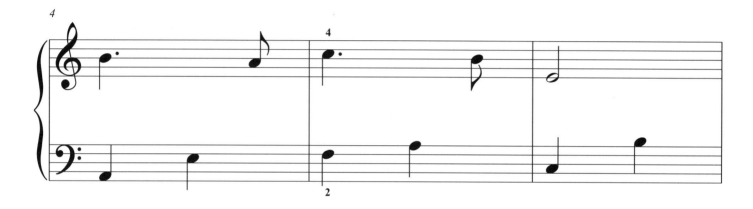

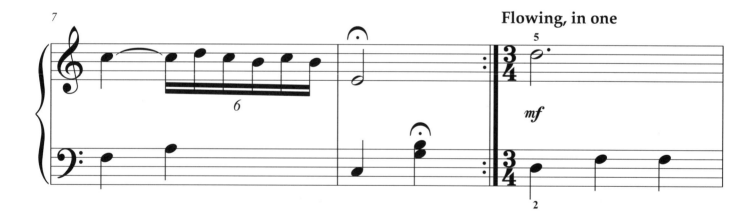

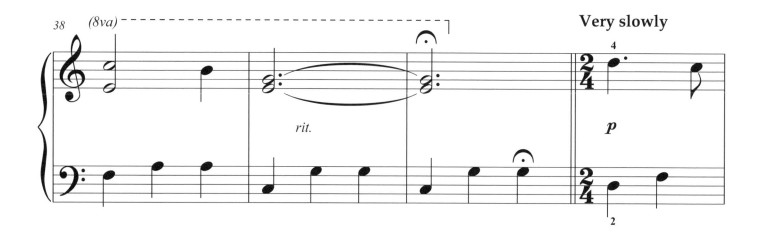

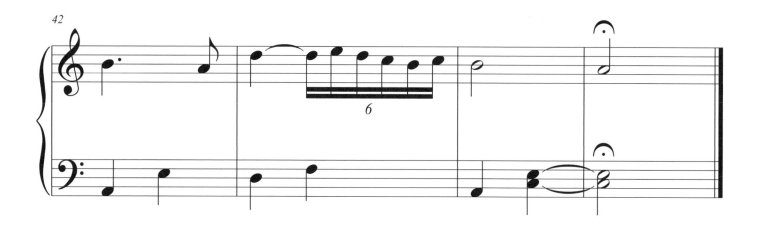

Misty

Music by ERROLL GARNER

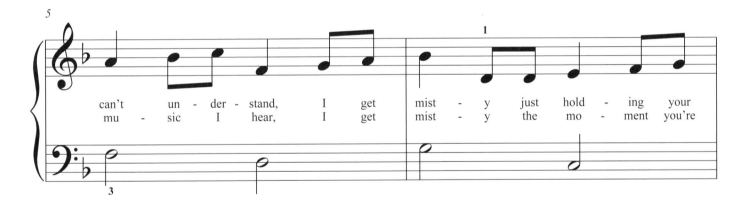

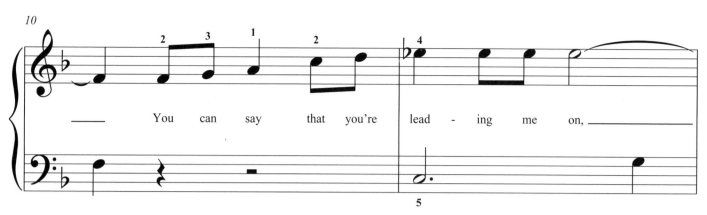

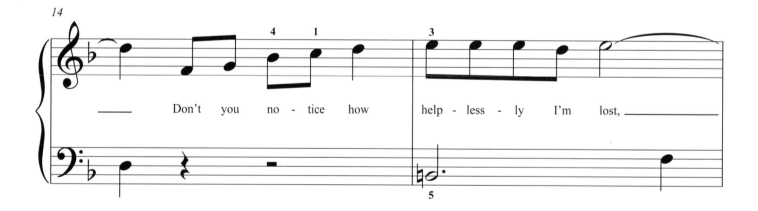

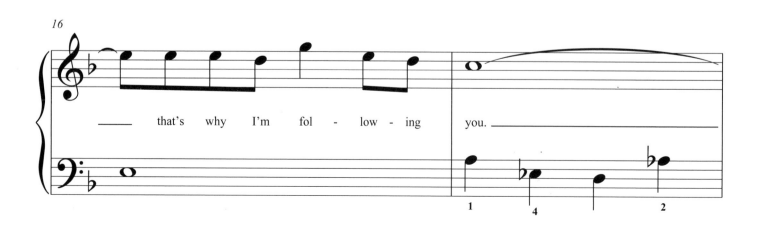

Lullabye
(Goodnight, My Angel)

Words and Music by
BILLY JOEL

Gently

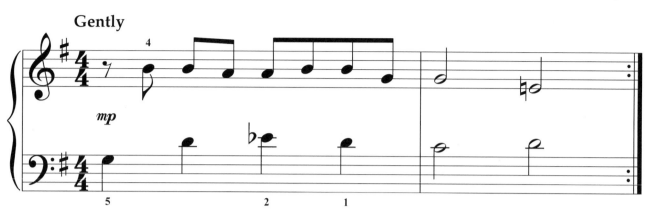

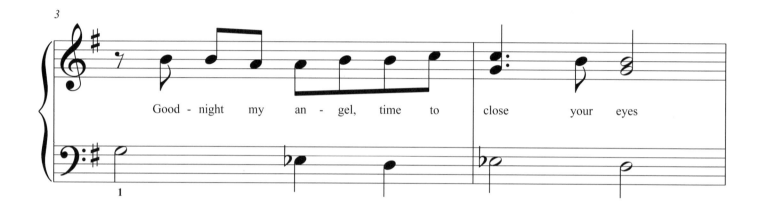

Good - night my an - gel, time to close your eyes

and save these ques - tions for an - oth - er day.

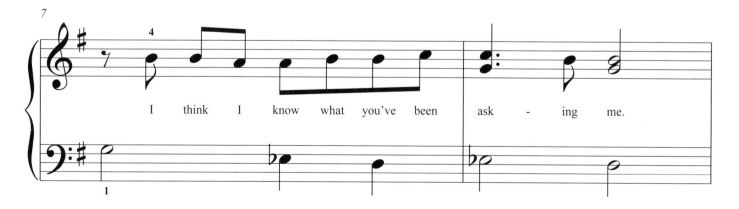

I think I know what you've been ask - ing me.

I think you know what I've been try'n' to say.

I prom - ised I would nev - er leave _____ you

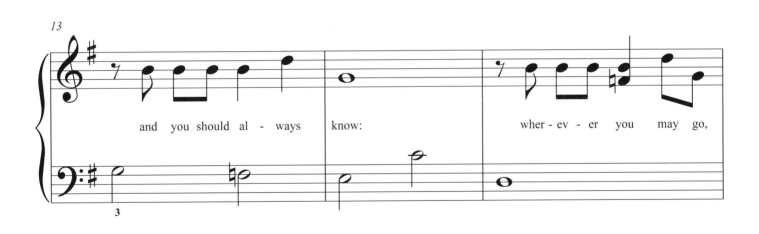

and you should al - ways know: wher - ev - er you may go,

no mat - ter where you are, I nev - er will be

far a-way. Good-night my an-gel, now it's time to dream

and dream how won-der-ful your life will be.

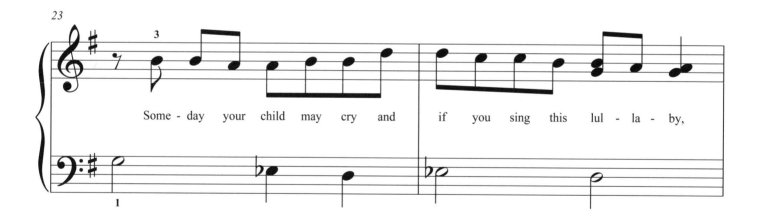

Some-day your child may cry and if you sing this lul-la-by,

then in your heart there will al-ways be a part of

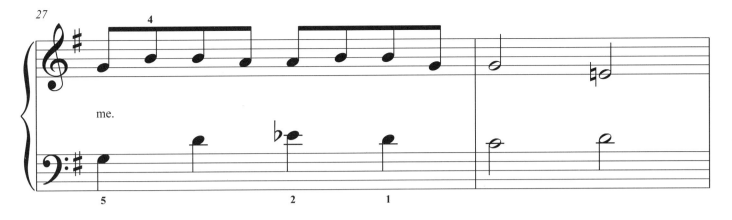

me.

Some - day we'll all be gone, but lul - la - bies go on and on.

They nev - er die. That's how you and _____ I will

be. *rit.*

Only Time

from SWEET NOVEMBER

Words and Music by ENYA,
NICKY RYAN and ROMA RYAN

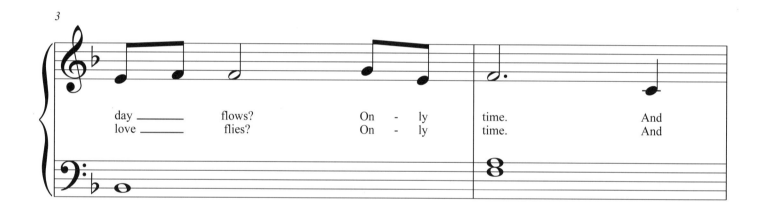

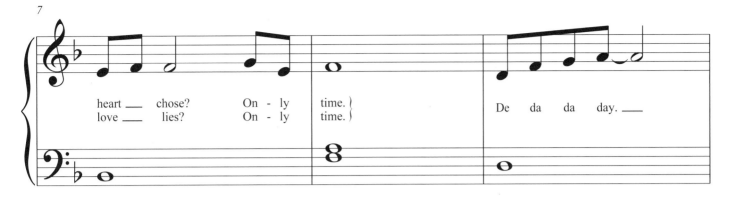

heart ___ chose?　　On - ly　time.
love ___ lies?　　On - ly　time.

De　da　da　day. ___

De　da　da　day. ___　　De　da　day.

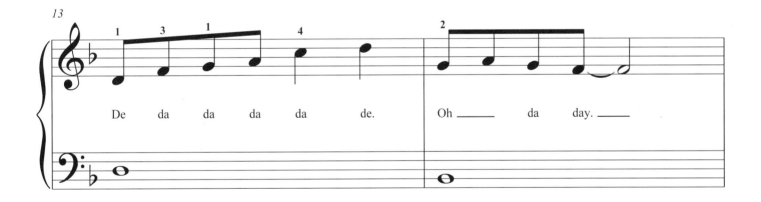

De　da　da　da　da　de.　　Oh ___ da　day. ___

De　da　da　day ___ da　day.　　Who　can　say　if　your

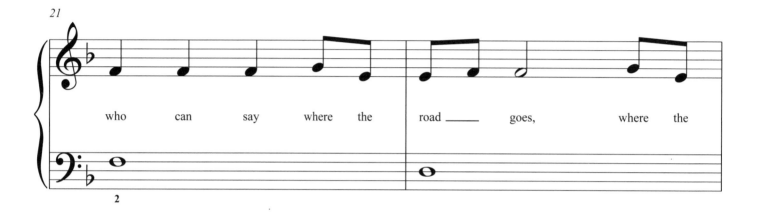

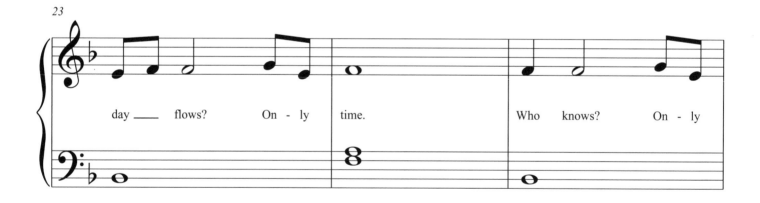

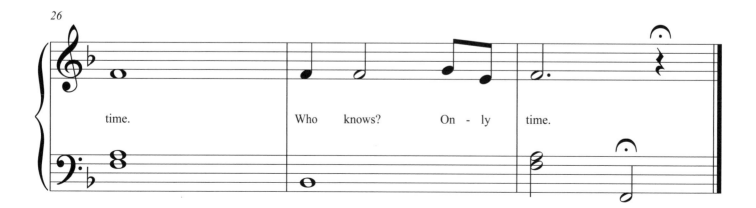

One Last Wish

from CASPER

By JAMES HORNER

Moderately

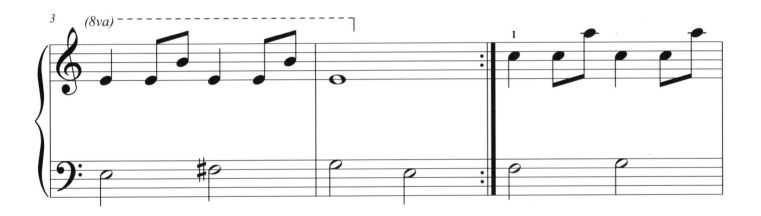

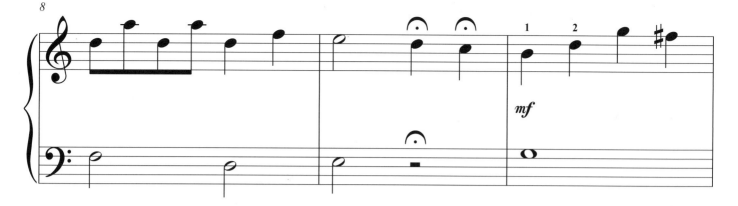

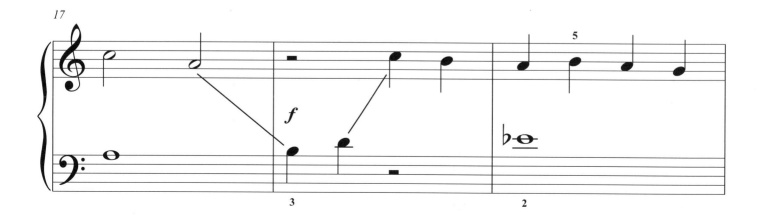

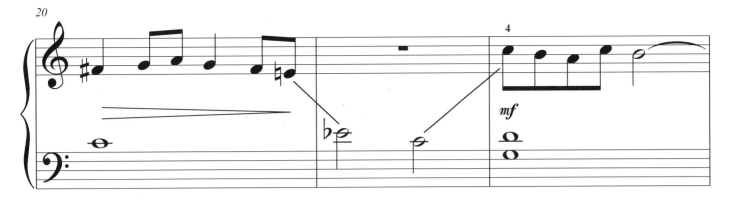

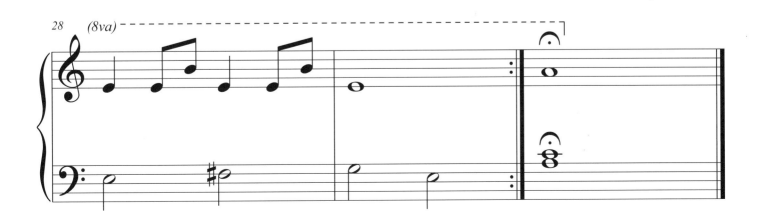

Skating

from A CHARLIE BROWN CHRISTMAS

By VINCE GUARALDI

Bright Jazz Waltz

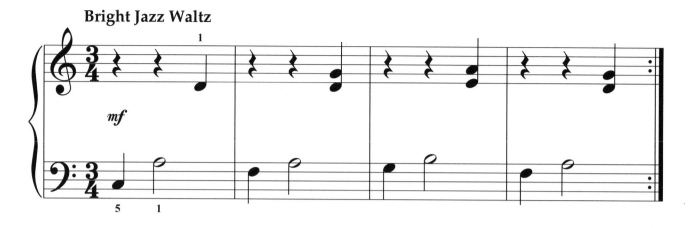

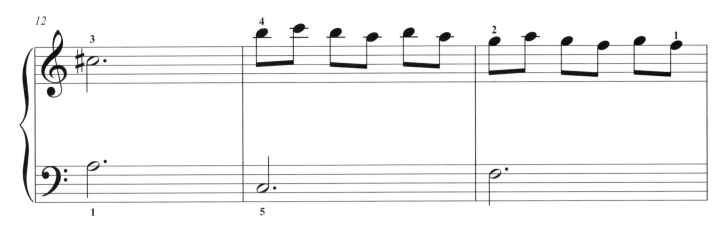

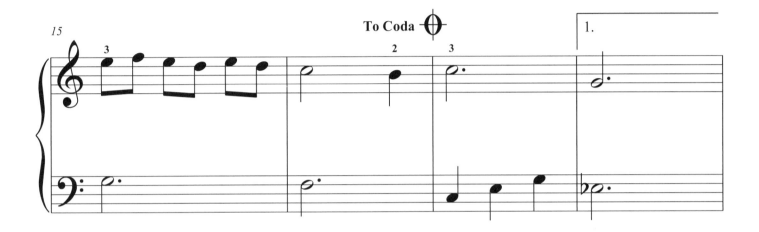

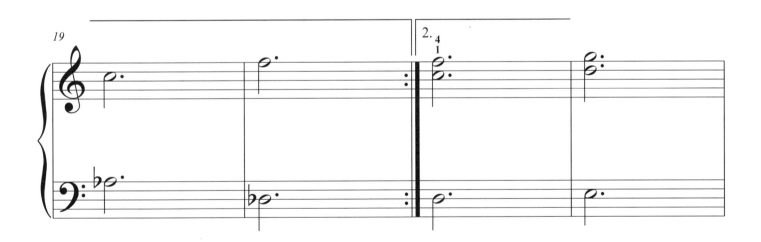

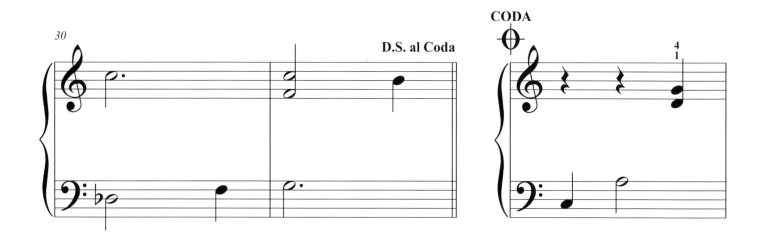

One Summer's Day
from SPIRITED AWAY

By JOE HISAISHI

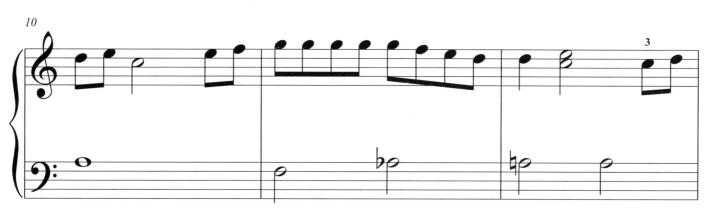

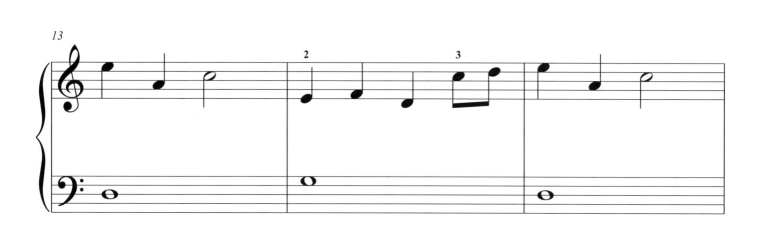

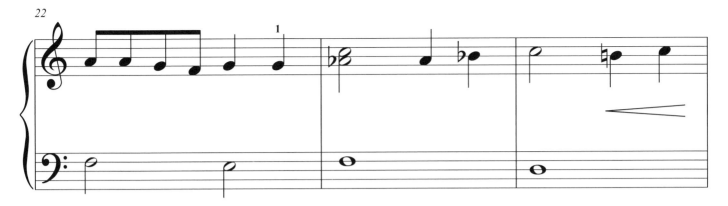

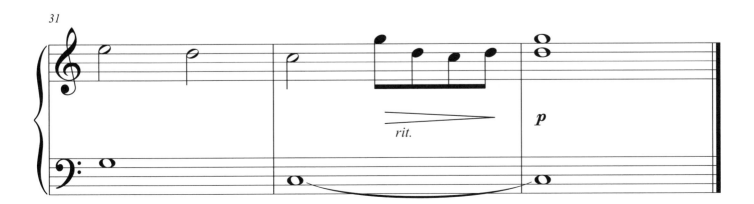

Song from a Secret Garden

By ROLF LØVLAND

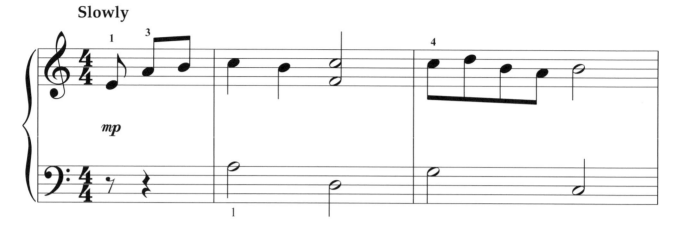

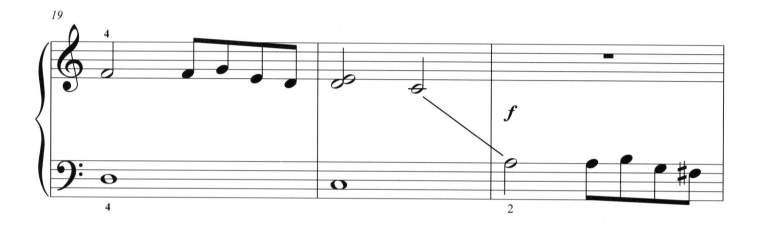

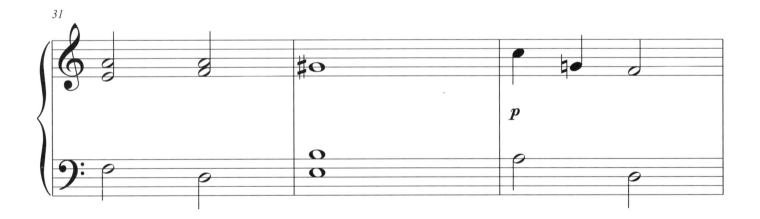

It's super easy! This series features accessible arrangements for piano, with simple right-hand melody, letter names inside each note, and basic left-hand chord diagrams. Perfect for players of all ages!

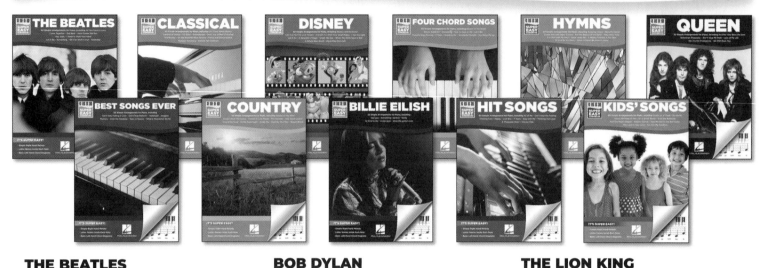

THE BEATLES
00198161 60 songs $15.99

BEAUTIFUL BALLADS
00385162 50 songs $14.99

BEETHOVEN
00345533 21 selections $9.99

BEST SONGS EVER
00329877 60 songs $16.99

BROADWAY
00193871 60 songs $15.99

JOHNNY CASH
00287524 20 songs $9.99

CHART HITS
00380277 24 songs $12.99

CHRISTMAS CAROLS
00277955 60 songs $15.99

CHRISTMAS SONGS
00236850 60 songs $15.99

CHRISTMAS SONGS WITH 3 CHORDS
00367423 30 songs $10.99

CLASSIC ROCK
00287526 60 songs $15.99

CLASSICAL
00194693 60 selections $15.99

COUNTRY
00285257 60 songs $15.99

DISNEY
00199558 60 songs $15.99

BOB DYLAN
00364487 22 songs $12.99

BILLIE EILISH
00346515 22 songs $10.99

FOLKSONGS
00381031 60 songs $15.99

FOUR CHORD SONGS
00249533 60 songs $15.99

FROZEN COLLECTION
00334069 14 songs $10.99

GEORGE GERSHWIN
00345536 22 songs $9.99

GOSPEL
00285256 60 songs $15.99

HIT SONGS
00194367 60 songs $16.99

HYMNS
00194659 60 songs $15.99

JAZZ STANDARDS
00233687 60 songs $15.99

BILLY JOEL
00329996 22 songs $10.99

ELTON JOHN
00298762 22 songs $10.99

KIDS' SONGS
00198009 60 songs $15.99

LEAN ON ME
00350593 22 songs $9.99

THE LION KING
00303511 9 songs $9.99

ANDREW LLOYD WEBBER
00249580 48 songs $19.99

MOVIE SONGS
00233670 60 songs $15.99

PEACEFUL MELODIES
00367880 60 songs $16.99

POP SONGS FOR KIDS
00346809 60 songs $16.99

POP STANDARDS
00233770 60 songs $16.99

QUEEN
00294889 20 songs $10.99

ED SHEERAN
00287525 20 songs $9.99

SIMPLE SONGS
00329906 60 songs $15.99

STAR WARS (EPISODES I-IX)
00345560 17 songs $10.99

TAYLOR SWIFT
00323195 22 songs $10.99

THREE CHORD SONGS
00249664 60 songs $15.99

TOP HITS
00300405 22 songs $10.99

WORSHIP
00294871 60 songs $15.99

Disney characters and artwork TM & © 2021 Disney

www.halleonard.com

Prices, contents and availability subject to change without notice.